Social Media and Intercultural Communication

Table of Contents

Our social tools are not an improvement to modern society, they are a challenge to it.

— Clay Shirky

Chapter 1. Introduction

Dive into the riveting domain of intercultural exchange with our Special Report on Social Media and Intercultural Communication! In an era where global connectivity is just a click away, understanding the impact and implications of our digital interactions is more important than ever. We span geographies and cultural divides, shedding light on the rainbow of human expression and weaving it into a vibrant tapestry of insights. This report spins a captivating narrative that is both intriguing and deeply relevant, born to pique your curiosity and expand your horizons. Uncover the symphony of global voices, discover the ripples of digital diplomacy, and navigate the depths of cultural nuance with us. Have your passport ready; our Special Report is your ticket to an unforgettable journey into the heart of the new age of communication! This is not just an opportunity to learn - it's a chance to understand the world better, in all its colorful diversity, one digital handshake at a time. So why just read, when you can explore? Embrace the call to adventure - pick up this Special Report today!

Chapter 2. Unfolding the Digital Tapestry: An Introduction to Social Media and Intercultural Communication

The realm of the digital age has been transformative in its scope, but none more so than the rapidly evolving domain of social media and intercultural communication. This chapter is designed to map out a framework that enhances understanding of the rich tapestry of cultures that interact with one another on online platforms, weaving a complex network of digital communities knitted together by shared connections and common discourses.

2.1. The Dawn of Social Media

In the realm of communications, the digital revolution has been nothing short of a meteoric rise. Sites like Facebook, Instagram, Twitter, and LinkedIn, as well as messaging apps like WhatsApp, have pervaded every demographic, becoming an essential part of everyday life. In a matter of years, these platforms have transformed from fringe novelties to integrated aspects of our personal and professional lives, fulfilling varied needs from emotional catharsis to practical communication. Our digital lives often mirror, and even influence, realities offline. The virtual world, with its millions of interwoven networks, is an ethnographer's dream and a linguist's playground.

2.2. The Intertwining of Cultures

Never before have global citizens been so intricately connected and mutually interdependent. The Internet's rise, coupled with advancements in translation technology and the widespread adoption of English as a lingua franca, have given birth to a new era of intercultural communication. The ideologies, perspectives, and insights that span cultures and continents are exchanged, debated, and synthesized in an instant, creating a dynamic melting pot of global knowledge and understanding.

2.3. The Power and Complexity of Intercultural Communication

Intercultural communication involves more than just language proficiency. It relates to an understanding of cultural nuances, values, and norms, the acknowledgment of power structures and colonial hangovers, and the sensitivity to various degrees of cultural openness or conservatism. Online platforms present an overlay of digital culture onto this already complex interaction, with platform-specific rules, etiquettes, algorithms, and trends.

Understanding this interplay is not an effortless task. Digital environments and their cues are often implicit and at times even cryptic. They are governed by a sense of digital citizenship, often understood and abided by users of the respective platform. The labyrinthine complexity of underscoring ideologies, value systems, power dynamics, and cultural encodings is made more intricate by the rapid pace at which digital trends change.

2.4. Social Media as a Cultural Mirror

Navigating this world is not simply a matter of understanding others. It is also about perceiving how others understand us. Our digital behavior - what we post, share, like, and comment on - creates digital images or personas of us in the minds of others. The collective image of a community or country is shaped by aggregated digital behaviors of its netizens, an effect that warrants just as much analysis and scrutiny.

Furthermore, the very definition of culture itself is under review. Traditionally understood in a geographical or regional sense, real and virtual overlap has led to the emergence of digital cultures. Subgroups within mainstream platforms - such as fan communities, professional groups on LinkedIn, meme sharers, or specific hashtag users - become their unique cultures with shared lingo, collective memories, traditions, and even hierarchies.

2.5. Looking Forward

Entering the world of social media and intercultural communication is akin to stepping into a hotel of babel, where hundreds of languages, ideologies, and cultures intersect. Understanding this intricate network can be complex, daunting even. But it is essential, especially in an age when differences in culture and perspective can be bridges of understanding rather than barriers.

Indeed, as we penetrate deeper into the Digital Age, existing methods of communication are likely to be further disrupted, and a digital glossary is all but sure to expand. Nevertheless, a principle tenet of this age, one that will likely outlast even the most futuristic changes, is the necessity for intercultural fluency in the face of swift, unanticipated shifts in how people communicate and understand one another, both offline and online.

With that, we invite you to join us as we venture deeper into the transformative domain of social media and intercultural communication. This is not a passive journey; it's a chance to be a digital anthropologist, uncovering the nuances and complexities of our connected world. Welcome, then, to a new age of understanding and exploration, where boundaries blur, cultures meld, and the world comes alive in a flurry of digital expression.

Chapter 3. The Global Village: Understanding our Digitally Connected World

In an age where assigning countries to continents may no longer be as feasible as assigning connections across the joint channels of digital communication, comprehending this newfound world village becomes of paramount importance. The term 'Global Village' was first coined by Marshall McLuhan, the noted philosopher of communication theory, in the 1960s. He predicted the internet-enabled, interconnected world we live in today long before the advent of digital technology on the scale we witness. Today, his vision rings truer than ever. Understanding the intricacies and implications of our rapidly shrinking global village is what gives us a lens into our digitally connected world.

3.1. The Internet: A Global Neighborhood

The internet has transformed the planet into a global locality, a single, continuously bustling neighborhood within our cyber realms. The everyday activities carried out on the internet transcend the cultural, geographic, and political borders that traditionally dictate interactions. Consider a high school student in Tokyo learning about the French Revolution from a digital class being broadcast in Paris. Or, consider the young entrepreneur in Accra who, due to the wonders of the internet, now has the opportunity to collaborate with a Swedish company to import and distribute eco-friendly products in Ghana. These instances are not mere hypotheticals but landmark examples of the transformative power of the internet, breaking down barriers, opening new opportunities, and bringing distant worlds closer together.

3.2. Social Media: The Interactive Agora

Among the many elements that contribute to this global neighborhood, social media is perhaps the most illustrious. Traditionally, our means of interaction were extensive and often one-directional, be it through television, radio, newspapers, or other media. Social media, however, allows for interaction and engagement on a multilateral, global scale, transforming passive audiences into active participants. It provides a platform where opinions from all corners of the earth can mingle, ideas can clash, and consensus can emerge.

Just as the ancient Greeks would gather in the agora for public debate or discussions, the social media platforms of today behave similarly. Facebook's news feeds, Twitter's timelines, Instagram's photo streams - they all serve as contemporary agoras where citizens of this digital global village gather for exchange.

3.3. Interconnectedness and Shared Cultures: A Mosaic

As people from different cultural backgrounds interact on these platforms, they influence and shape each other's cultures. This shared shaping paves the way for a global culture, a mosaic created from a myriad of local cultures all intersecting through the rubric of digital communication. People the world over are experiencing cultural osmosis – the movies of Hollywood as much a part of the Indian viewer's experience as the Bollywood films are of an avid American moviegoer's.

This is not to argue that local cultures are being washed away in a tsunami of dominant cultures. Rather, it's to acknowledge that through access and exposure to foreign cultures, local cultures are being enriched and augmented, like a tapestry woven with threads from every corner of the globe.

3.4. Cyber Politics: Governing the Digital World

Moreover, as the digital world continues expanding, so too must our understanding of its system of governance. Rules, regulations, and laws that function seamlessly in the physical world may fall short in addressing problems unique to the internet. Cyberbullying, identity theft, data protection – these are all matters we must collectively address under the mantle of cyber politics.

As we create a global village online, parallel systems of justice, equity, and participation need to be considered and implemented. This is not a trivial task as it involves taking into account the cultural sensitivities, beliefs, and values of different regions, and doing so in a way that champions universal human rights.

3.5. The Road Ahead: Shaping Our Digital Future

The future of our global village appears vibrant and limitless. With technology continually growing and evolving, so too are the ways in which we interact with one another. As we continue to learn, connect, share, and grow on these platforms, it is crucial that we recognize the innate power and influence this has on our intercultural relations. And as we inch towards tomorrow, it becomes incumbent upon us to use our interconnectedness responsibly, and work towards a digital society that is inclusive, diverse, and empowering for all.

In conclusion, this new interconnected era brings with it an array of opportunities and challenges. It offers the thrill of global interconnectedness, the union of diverse cultures, and the chance for everyday individuals to interact with the world at large. However, it also brings questions of personal identity, cultural sensitivity, and shared responsibility to the fore, demanding our attention, understanding, and action. As we navigate our way through our digitally connected global village, we ought to be mindful of the world we're shaping, for it is the legacy we are leaving to future citizens of this sprawling global neighborhood.

Chapter 4. Linguistic Variations in Social Media: A Close Examination

The advent of the age of social media has brought numerous implications for communication, with linguistic variations being one of the most fascinating facets. The rise of linguistic multiplicity has permeated global online communication, harnessing the willful enthusiasm of the digital-era participatory culture. This chapter provides an in-depth analysis and exploration of the linguistic diversities observed on various platforms, such as Facebook, Twitter, Instagram, and more.

4.1. Linguistic Patterns and Social Media's Global Impact

Employing a global lens, we can first determine that the global headway of social media has propelled a distinctive shift from monolingual to multilingual communication. With social media networks hosting an assortment of languages, from primary world languages to smaller regional dialects, there exists a vibrant dyad of global and local linguistic tones. The global-local dyad is indeed reflective of the unending ebb and flow of cultural exchange and communication in our digital world.

In countries where multilingualism is the norm, there presents a unique linguistic phenomenon—code-switching, or the practice of alternating between two or more languages or linguistic varieties in conversation. Within the digital landscapes of social media, code-switching frequently occurs, frequently showcasing the user's cultural versatility or social niche.

The use of non-standard linguistic elements also sees an emergence as a dominant pattern on social media platforms. The employment of abbreviations, acronyms, and slang is a testament to the dynamic and evolving nature of linguistic practices on social media.

4.2. Language, Identity and Micro-style in Social Media

The relationship between language and identity is evident and palpable in most, if not all, digital communities. Social media users wield linguistic styles as tools for establishing personal and group identities. Linguistic style in this context refers to a peculiar set of linguistic features, grammar, vocabulary, and pronunciation, used consistently by a social media user. This unique digital fingerprint, characterized as 'micro-style', creates a sense of belonging and camaraderie among users.

Multimodality, a central tenet of micro-style, introduces an array of communicative modes beyond just text. This includes photographs, videos, emojis, stickers, and memes among others. These elements, often used in combination, effectively establish a more nuanced, comprehensive form of online communication that engages users on a deeper, emotional level.

4.3. Emojis: The Universal Language in Social Media

Possessing a shared language helps bond communities, and in the context of the digital world, emojis have emerged as a semi-universal, semi-standardized language. Emojis transcend the boundaries of written languages, offering a simple, colorful, and evocative mean to convey emotions, ideas, and actions across different cultures.

Emojis, in their silent resonance, play a dual role. They act as a surrogate for physical cues such as facial expressions that are absent in text-based interaction. Concurrently, they serve as speech acts, a linguistic term referring to utterances that perform a function.

4.4. The Role of Artificial Intelligence (AI) in Detecting Linguistic Variation

Artificial Intelligence has revolutionized the way we detect, analyze, and understand linguistic variations on social media platforms. Natural language processing (NLP), a subfield of AI, plays a key role in interpreting user-generated content, which can be incredibly diverse in terms of syntax, semantics, and dialect.

Machine learning algorithms trained to evaluate data at various levels—syntactic, semantic, or discourse—have exhibited profound proficiency in detecting linguistic variations that would have otherwise gone unnoticed to the naked eye.

The algorithms are designed to learn from a massive dataset of social media language usage, identify trends and patterns, and interpret linguistic variations with unprecedented efficiency, contributing to data-driven insights into language use in digital discourse.

In conclusion, the realm of social media continues to serve as a compelling platform that blends linguistic variations with innovative communication practices. With global, regional, and cultural influences impacting the narratives, a rich tapestry of linguistic diversity emerges online, reflecting the colorful, multi-hued spectrum of human communication. Social media offers a treasure trove of insights into the emerging complexities of intercultural communication in our increasingly connected global village, making this an exciting area of exploration for linguists and cultural scholars alike.

Chapter 5. Emojis, Memes and Gifs: The Universal Language of the Internet

In this digital epoch, where arguably every human emotion can be encapsulated by a simplistic emoji, memes harmonize humor across cultures and GIFs interject dynamism into static screen conversations, we delve into the fascinating realm of these non-verbal digital languages that personify the creation, interpretation, and exchange of meaning on the ubiquitous landscape of the Internet.

5.1. The Alphabet of Emoticons

In the sprawling metropolis of the World Wide Web, text often falters to communicate the subtle nuances of human emotion. Here, emojis or emoticons, originally invented in Japan in the 1990s, play the role of global digital ambassadors, brokering understanding across linguistic barriers. They epitomize the 'picture speaks a thousand words' adage, encapsulating complex emotions into compact digital images - a heart for love, a smiley for joy, a frown for dismay—the list could hold you engrossed indefinitely.

Consider the populous virtual arenas of Facebook and Instagram. Every like, love, laugh, shock, or sad reaction opens up new perspectives into how different individuals react and respond to a single piece of content. It's a demonstration of empathy, an assertion of mutual understanding, and at times, a simple show of digital solidarity.

5.2. Memes – Humour in Bytes

Next, we navigate through the labyrinth of memes – digital humor expressed as an idea, behavior, style, or usage that spreads from person to person within a culture. Borrowed from evolutionary biology, the term 'Meme' finds its modern connotation in the realm of cyberspace where it has created its distinct footprint. A meme represents and molds public sentiment, conveying criticism, parody, and wit within a single visual or textual representation.

While a meme's content varies across cultures, the essence of humor it carries is largely universal. One could be tickled by the wit of a meme born thousands of miles away, bearing no relation to one's roots. Indeed, memes offer insights into different cultural contexts to those residing beyond their geographical origins.

5.3. GIFs – Lending Motion to Expression

Fast forward to the dynamic world of Graphics Interchange Format or GIFs. Born in the late 1980s, GIFs have transformed the way we communicate in the online universe. Combining multiple images or 'frames' in a single file, GIFs are able to encapsulate seconds of motion - a stark contrast against the static world of text and images.

GIFs effectively represent cultures, their peculiarities, and idiosyncrasies, lending impressionable insight into their nuances. Catchphrases, societal trends, pop culture symbols - every cultural artifact manifests within GIFs, extending the global understanding and appreciation of diverse cultures.

5.4. Crossing Cultural Barriers

While emojis, memes, and GIFs independently offer their unique contributions, they unite in their function as a universal key, unlocking cultural gates across the digital expanse. Each communicates a part of the human experience, and when seen on a global scale, it demonstrates how similar we all are despite disparate cultural backgrounds. By providing everyone with succinct and relatable expressions of thought and feeling, these digital constructs ensure that no culture is truly isolated in this age of connectivity.

5.5. Navigating Misinterpretation

Despite their beneficial role, emojis, memes, and GIFs pose certain challenges in intercultural communication. Misinterpretations, occasionally leading to diplomatic tensions in the virtual realm, underscore the necessary careful and tactful deployment of these digital tools. As with any language, comprehension requires a nuanced understanding of its syntax, grammar and the cultural connotation, raising the pressing need for digital literacy.

To conclude, emojis, memes, and GIFs contribute immensely to a universal language that transcends borders. With appropriate sensibility and mutual respect, these digital elements continue their voyage, navigating the Internet's ceaseless currents, shaping the course of intercultural communication in this digital era. Their journey underlines the essence of global connectivity - a dance of words and images worth partaking in, a shared language that thrives on the vibrant diversity of human experience. Ironically, by saying less, they often communicate so much more.

This in-depth exploration offers food for thought and inevitably, leaves one marveling at the exponential potential these dynamic, digital languages hold in fostering global understanding and stimulating an enriching exchange of cultural flavors in our digitized world. Their potential is vast, and as long as humans have the impetus to communicate and connect – irrespective of geography, culture, or creed – this universal language of the internet will continue to evolve and thrive. Satellite by satellite, server by server, and heart by emoji heart.

Chapter 6. The Power of Hashtags: Uniting Voices Across Cultures

Brace yourselves, dear readers, as we embark on an intellectual journey exploring the impact of hashtags in the realm of intercultural communication. In the dynamic and fast-paced world of social media, the hashtag has ascended to a prominent status. Through it, we observe an impressive feat of uniting voices across cultures. But to truly grasp the power of hashtags entails reading the signs and discerning the stories resting beneath their emblematic pound symbol.

6.1. The Hashtag: An Internet Age Hieroglyph

Allow us, first, to delve into the genesis of the hashtag—an amalgam of the English word 'hash' (referring to the pound symbol '#') and 'tag' (a term derived from tagging artifacts on the internet). When the Internet was fairly nascent, the hashtag hadn't yet arrived on the digital stage. It was first used on August 23, 2007, by Chris Messina, a social media specialist whose infamous tweet, "how do you feel about using # (pound) for groups. As in #barcamp [msg]?" made history. This innocuous symbol, formerly consigned to programming languages, now has its celebrated status as a defining feature of our increasingly digital lives.

Initially introduced on Twitter, this potent tool quickly spread to the likes of Instagram, Facebook, LinkedIn, and many other networking platforms, becoming a global phenomenon. Facilitating a new style of intercultural communication, hashtags have evolved far beyond sorting posts into categories; they've become rallying cries for globally relevant issues and bridge linguistic divides.

6.2. Harnessing Hashtags for Cross-Cultural Conversation

Before zooming in on how this occurs, let's unravel some of the core functions of hashtags. At the most basic level, they categorize posts, allowing users to sift through the digital deluge fell upon us courtesy of modern social media. They connect posts across varied accounts, encapsulating global conversations in a single phrase or word preceded by a '#'. They're seen as expressways to trending topics, enabling anyone to engage in a larger dialogue.

Through this, hashtags offer unbounded opportunities for disparate individuals to transcend geopolitical, linguistic, and cultural frontiers connecting experiences, ideas, and movements worldwide. As we see instances such as #BlackLivesMatter or #PrayForParis trending, a powerful narrative unravels, uniting a multitude of voices across different cultures. Spirited discussions and shared empathy become epitomized in these hashtags, transforming them into global phenomena that tie us together in a web of shared humanity.

6.3. The Synergy of Language and Hashtags

Even when we shift our lens to the linguistic landscape, the depth of hashtags' influence is astounding. They act as a universal language, largely independent of the diverse tongues spoken across our planet's surface. By converging dialogue into concise, universally recognizable phrases or words, they effortlessly cross language barriers, facilitating cultural exchange of unprecedented proportions.

An interesting offshoot of this is the rise of multilingual and code-switching hashtags—terms that cleverly fuse two languages into one tag. A rallying cry like #YoTambien, blending Spanish and English languages, exemplifies this and turns the digital space into a melting pot of cultures and languages, echoing global solidarity and mutual understanding.

6.4. The Political Might of Hashtags

In the realm of politics, hashtags wield substantial influence as they have the ability to unite people for common causes overriding political orientations and national boundaries. Celebrated instances such as #ArabSpring and #MeToo, inter alia, highlighted the immense power of collective consciousness leveraged through hashtags, triggering revolutionary waves that transcended continents.

They've become instrumental in mobilizing global support, drawing attention to crucial matters, and even influencing policy-making decisions. As expressions of digital diplomacy, hashtags allow users to share stories, express opinions, and shape narratives on a global scale, thus allowing for more inclusive and representative intercultural exchanges.

6.5. Unveiling Cultural Nuances Through Hashtags

With the rise of hashtags, we've also witnessed a profound shift in how cultures are perceived and represented. They act as lighthouses, beckoning our attention towards varied cultural phenomena, be it the Korean #Hallyu wave or the love for Mexican food marked by #TacoTuesday.

These hashtags embody cultural nuances and idiosyncrasies, ultimately leading to a more comprehensive and authentic representation. By facilitating a communal sharing of cultural elements, they foster cultural appreciation and understanding, further blurring the lines of division drawn by geography and history.

6.6. Conclusion: The Hashtag, A Unifier

As we guide you to the end of this chapter, it is undeniable that the landscape of intercultural communication has been deeply enriched by the humble hashtag. Acting as signposts in the tumultuous world of social media, they've redefined the way we engage in global dialogues. Now a contemporary language that transcends borders, they hold the potential to unite mankind as never before.

Hashtags, in essence, are more than mere organizational tools. They've emerged as the rallying cries of generations, digital harbingers of social change, diplomatic bridges, and cultural explorers. They provide everyday citizens with the platform to contribute their voice to the global dialogue, amplifying issues and sentiments which might have previously slipped under the radar.

As we navigate the world of social media and intercultural communication, the profound resonance of the hashtag remains a testament to the transformative power of digital discourse, underlining our shared experience of life, in all its vibrant and diverse forms. Breathe, observe, and engage: be part of this transformative journey, one hashtag at a time. After all, isn't it remarkable that something as simple as a # can bear such implications and change the trajectory of our shared human experience? Let this lingering thought guide you as you traverse the subsequent chapters of this book.

Chapter 7. Social Media Diplomacy: Bridging the Political Divide

In an era where the murmurs of keyboards echo louder than the spoken word, the role of social media diplomacy emerges profound and vitally relevant. It's a lifeline that we have extended across the world, offering an olive branch of understanding, empathy, and collaboration. As diplomats of our time scramble to adapt to this new landscape, we must also appreciate the nuances within it - investigating the potential pitfalls and promises that ride along with this digital revolution.

7.1. Harnessing the Power of Social Media in Diplomacy

Diplomacy has historically been the exclusive domain of well-groomed statesmen and envoys who communicated through official channels, carefully worded speeches, and elaborate dinners. Social media, in its relative childhood, has provided an upheaval to these ivory towers. It provides a platform for a more democratic, accessible, and real-time diplomacy. World leaders and diplomats utilize Twitter, Facebook, Instagram, and LinkedIn as tools of persuasion, engagement, and influence. They tweet, post photos, share opinions, and in doing so, communicate directly and articulately with the masses. It is a method of diplomatic engagement that is transparent, instantaneous, and interactive.

With over 3.6 billion active social media users worldwide, the strategies of direct engagement and shaping public discourse are transforming how diplomacy is undertaken. The digital age requires both traditional players in international affairs and the public to develop a nuanced understanding of the digital landscape and its potential, leveraging these tools to bridge political divides and foster collective action.

7.2. The Pragmatics of Digital Diplomacy

An essential aspect of digital diplomacy is the pragmatics behind its usage. It is not enough to communicate; careful attention needs to be paid to how the communication is conducted. An understanding of the audience and the cultivation of the message accordingly is of paramount importance. The choice of platform is also crucial. For instance, LinkedIn conveys a more professional demeanor while Instagram offers a more personal perspective into a diplomat's work and personal life.

In the age of information overload, the formulation of concise yet impactful policy narratives becomes vitally essential. The usage of precise and powerful hashtags can coalesce communities around a common cause. The generation of online conversations invites a broader participation base, thereby meeting diplomacy's primary aim - reaching consensus.

Another engaging aspect of digital diplomacy is the usage of cultural references, memes, and even emojis. This shared cultural currency can make the communication more relatable, approachable, and even humorous - humanizing the otherwise formalized facet of diplomacy.

7.3. Challenges and Pitfalls of Digital Diplomacy

While the digital medium has advantages, it is not without its challenges. Diplomats need to navigate a minefield of trolls, fake news, and the risk of their messages being lost in the digital noise. It can also lead to a dilution of official stances, forcing diplomats to manage both offline and online repercussions. Privacy concerns and the potential breach of security are further risks in this digital landscape.

7.4. Real-world Cases of Digital Diplomacy

A few key real-world examples further illustrate the impact of digital diplomacy. The Arab Spring is such an instance where social media played a significant role in mobilizing people. Barack Obama's extensive usage of Facebook during his electoral campaign and Narendra Modi's adept use of Twitter are prime examples of how leaders have effectively harnessed the medium.

7.5. Towards a More Connected Future

Digital diplomacy, despite its challenges, offers a path towards fostering better international relationships. It allows a space for dialogue, a reaching of consensus across borders, and promotes transparency. As we march further into the digital age, we must gear toward a responsible usage, leveraging it to bridge the political divide, and facilitate cooperation and mutual understanding.

In conclusion, social media diplomacy is a powerful tool with the potential to rebuild the shape of international discourse. Its proper harnessing is dependent on the willingness of diplomats, world leaders, and the public to adapt, learn and mature with this rapidly evolving medium. As the world grows smaller with each WhatsApp message or Instagram post, our global village seems more real than ever, building peace, one tweet at a time.

Chapter 8. Online Identity and Cultural Representation: The Role of Social Media

With the burgeoning advent of social media, the integral role it plays in fostering online identities, subsequently creating a direct impact on overall cultural representation has become impossible to ignore. This chapter seeks to expound on this significant aspect, delving into deeper layers and intricacies like never before.

8.1. Fostering Online Identities

The process of forming an online identity begins with the user's interaction with social media platforms. Whether it's posting updates on Facebook, sharing pictures on Instagram, tweeting on Twitter, or networking on LinkedIn, our online persona emerges from every virtual utterance and action. It's the essence distilled from our digital footprint — the comments we pen, the posts we like or share, the photos we upload, the hashtags we use. Each of these elements nurtures signals, grappling together to form our narrative in the online sphere.

Not limited to personal expression, our digital identities also echo our cultural affiliations. The symbols, language, and nuances unique to one's cultural backdrop seep into our online personas, painting a vivid image of our cultural milieu. For instance, the use of particular vernaculars or local idioms, the celebration of regional events, or expression of native customs and practices, all find a way into our digital expression, providing a dynamic view of our cultural spectrums.

8.2. The Impact on Cultural Representation

Building upon this complex intersection of personal and cultural identity online, it's essential to highlight the profound impact this has on cultural representation. Traditional channels of cultural exchange were often limited in scope, prone to distortion, or mired in prejudice, engendering a skewed presentation of cultural diversity. However, swimming in the current of digital revolution, social media channels surface as a beacon of democratized cultural representation.

In the faceless world of social media, what stands out above all, is the kaleidoscope of cultures in the individual's possession. Be it a small Midwestern town, a bustling megacity in Asia, or a quiet pastoral corner of Europe, online platforms provide a stage for communities from all walks of life to relay their unique cultural narratives.

Micro-blogging platforms like Twitter, image-based mediums like Instagram, or short video platforms like TikTok, each harness their distinctive nature, aiding users in highlighting the richness, the diversity, and the nuance of their respective cultural identities. Hashtags like #CultureGully, #MyCultureMyPride, or micro-trends emerging from regions lesser-known, contribute to a digital milieu that is accepting, intuitive, and representative of a vast array of worldwide cultures.

Moreover, social media platforms furnish users with an agency that traditional media seldom permits. Individual voices, now armed with the liberating power of self-publication, pave the way for authentic showcase of lesser-represented cultures and minority communities.

8.3. Challenges and Considerations

However, the path to representational utopia is not devoid of obstacles. Cultural appropriation, digital disparity, and the possibility of offensive misunderstandings do lurk within the corners of online interaction. Inaccurate artifacts or caricatures of cultures can easily circulate, leading to misconceptions. Therefore, it falls upon the users, both as content creators and consumers, to ensure due diligence and respect for cultural sensitivities.

Despite these potential pitfalls, the role of social media in shaping online identities and cultural representation remains overwhelmingly constructive, particularly when paired with responsible usage and respectful digital citizenship. It serves to empower us, allowing us to choose how we present ourselves and our cultures on a global stage, thereby cultivating a worldwide forum of diverse, inclusive dialogue.

In conclusion, the journey from the formation of online identities to their impact on cultural representation, steered by the omnipresent force of social media, is a fascinating voyage of human and cultural understanding. Life within the spectrum of digital technology and social media indeed represents an epochal shift in shaping self-expression, breaking down barriers, fostering cultural representation, and relentless human connection. The discourse presented here unravels these engaging structures and is an ode to the power, as well as the probable pitfalls, of the cultural representation propagated by the global citizenry through social media.

Chapter 9. Glocalization of Content: The Intersection of Global and Local Cultures

In a world characterized by digital connectivity and the ceaseless flow of information, the overlap between local and global cultures has intensified, creating a unique phenomenon known as 'glocalization'. Stemming from an amalgamation of 'globalization' and 'localization', this term refers to the adoption of global ideas and practices into a local context, retaining the essence of the local culture while assimilating influences from across the world.

9.1. Embracing the Glocal Approach

In a glocalized world, the borders between the global and the local become porous, and yet each maintains its distinctive qualities. To give an example, consider the realm of entertainment. A Hollywood movie could be subtitled or dubbed in various languages, designed to cater to audiences worldwide. While the underlying narrative and themes of the movie remain fundamentally global, these localization adjustments ensure it resonates with local audiences, allowing them to engage with the story within their cultural context.

Meanwhile, social media plays a significant role as a marketplace for cultural exchange where this glocalization occurs. Platforms such as Facebook, Twitter, Instagram, and others function as virtual stages where the global and the local converge. Here, individual users bring their local experiences and perspectives to the table, while interacting with ideas, narratives, and content that has been globalized.

9.2. Social Media: The Great Equalizer

The internet has been termed a great democratizer, and rightly so. In the vast expanse of cyberspace, any user with the necessary digital tools and know-how can create content that can travel across borders. This has created space for smaller, localized cultures to project their unique narratives onto the global stage.

Take, for example, the surge in popularity of K-pop worldwide. This genre of music, originating from South Korea, is steeply rooted in Korean culture and language. However, artists such as BTS and Blackpink have gained unprecedented international followings. While the global audiences may not understand the language or nuances of Korean culture directly, the universal themes of love, struggle, heartbreak, and triumph in the music, combined with its distinctive musicality and performance aspects, have charmed listeners worldwide.

Simultaneously, these artists implement localized elements like English phrases in their lyrics, western beats, and international themes, engaging in a form of glocalization. By striking this balance, they successfully appeal to both domestic and international audiences, fostering cultural exchange and understanding in the process.

9.3. Glocalized Marketing Strategies

The business domain has been quick to recognize and leverage the power of glocalization for marketing. Brands like McDonald's, Starbucks, and Ikea have effectively implemented glocal strategies. They maintain their global brand identity while customizing products to match the preferences and tastes of local customers.

For example, McDonald's, a quintessentially American brand, offers the Maharaja Mac in India, the Teriyaki McBurger in Japan, and the McArabia in the Middle East. These products cater to the flavors and food habits of these regions, while still being served under the umbrella of a global brand. Thus, social media platforms, with their immense reach, have become strategic tools in executing these glocalized marketing campaigns, allowing these brands to resonate with customers both globally and locally.

9.4. Glocalization in the Age of Digital Diplomacy

It is intriguing to see how the concept of glocalization translates into the realm of social and political discourse. For example, consider political movements that, while rooted in specific local contexts, have garnered global attention and support on social media. The Black Lives Matter movement began in the United States but resonated with audiences worldwide, with rallies being held in different parts of the world.

The movement's core message, addressing systemic racism, was a distinctly local issue, yet it struck a chord with international audiences, leading to global solidarity. The localized content became globalized via social media, emphasizing the intertwined nature of local and global contexts in the digital age.

9.5. Towards a Glocalized Future

As we move forward, the wave of glocalization is poised to gain strength, powered by the unrelenting force of digitalization. As social media platforms continue to evolve and transform, they will continue to offer room for more narratives, voices, and cultures to merge into the global social stage.

Social media platforms also have a crucial role to play in ensuring equal representation, to balance the global with the local. By offering the necessary tools and platforms for localized communities and cultures to voice their stories, they can contribute significantly to fostering global unity in diversity.

In concluding, glocalization marks a new chapter in the narrative of cultural exchange and interaction. It combines the immense scope of global ideas with the richness and distinctiveness of local cultures, creating a vibrant, diverse, and cohesive global cultural scape. Social media, with its phenomenal reach and ability to cut across geographical and cultural divides, plays a pivotal role as a facilitator of glocal content exchange, turning the abstract concept of glocalization into a tangible, lived-in reality for millions of users around the globe.

Chapter 10. Overcoming Digital Disparity: Ensuring Equal Intercultural Representation

The spotlight of this crucial chapter moves ceaselessly over the textured landscape of digital disparity - the gaping fissures in the shining façade of global connectivity. It is indeed a tantalizing irony that in a digitized world, where even the most remote regions can theoretically be virtually linked, millions remain excluded from the dynamic digital discourse underway. This chapter boldly addresses this issue, presenting first the intricate complexities of the digital divide, then discussing potential solutions, and, ultimately, advocating for the formulation of an inclusive online landscape that is both multicultural and equitably representative.

10.1. Unmasking the Digital Divide

At a surface glance, the world seems awash with digital connections. We flit from status updates to viral memes, threaded discussions to live chats, our digital footprints extending across every conceivable social media platform. Yet this lively digital dance belies an underlying reality, a reality where not all are invited to the party. This omission is not arbitrary; it's systematic, born from a confluence of social, economic, and political factors all interlinked. Digital disparity, or what we commonly term as the 'digital divide', implicitly and explicitly hinders an equal representation of cultural inputs into the global communication landscape.

So, what does this divide look like? It constitutes disparities in access to digital infrastructure, lowered digital literacy rates, and underlying policy gaps that manifest in an inequitable provisioning of resources. It's crucial to note that these dimensions are not discrete, rather they exist in an intertwined form, reinforcing one another, deepening the divide and exacerbating digital disparity.

But where do we see these disparities play out? Disparities unfold across regional lines, with the global north often privy to superior digital access compared to their southern counterparts. They are visible across socio-economic strata, where prosperity often acts as a gatekeeper to digital access. They are gendered, disadvantaging women, particularly in developing nations, who lack requisite digital exposure. And they echo across the rural-urban chasm, with urban occupants often enjoying better digital access.

10.2. Bridging the Divide: Policy, Infrastructure, and Education

Drawing from research, eyewitness accounts, and study cases, the chapter next delves into the possible solutions that promise to bridge the digital chasm. The first arena we need to focus on is, of course, the policy framework. Legislation shapes the narrative, especially when it comes to distributing resources, including digital resources. The call for policies that ensure access to basic digital infrastructure such as reliable internet and digital tools, for everyone, is not just an ideal; it is an urgent requirement. These resources should be available universally, like other socio-economic goods, irrespective of geographical, economical, or sociopolitical identity.

Investments in digital infrastructure form a significant solution to the existing digital divide. Economically disadvantaged regions require focused attention on developing robust digital infrastructure that includes both hardware (devices, network infrastructure) and software (user-friendly interfaces, secure platforms). Simultaneously, high-speed, reliable internet should be treated as more than just a privilege; it should be a right assured to all citizens.

Education plays a paramount role in overcoming digital disparity. The demographic afflicted by lower digital literacy rates needs interventions designed to equip them with the necessary skills to navigate the digital realm. Digital education, therefore, needs to be integrated within the formal education channels, along with creating adult learning programmes for those who missed out early on digital learning opportunities.

10.3. The Way Forward: Advocacy, Collaboration, and Equal Opportunities

The overarching goal is to create an all-inclusive platform for intercultural communication, a digital sphere where every voice is heard, and every representation holds worth, a space where each global citizen has an equal opportunity to participate and contribute to the digital narrative.

As we peer into the future of social media and intercultural communication, we advocate for a twofold approach. First, a raised global consciousness to the existence of the digital divide, and second, consistent cooperation between governments, international bodies, private entities, non-governmental organizations, and communities to address it.

With consistent efforts and a shared vision, we can gradually reduce digital disparity and create an arena where intercultural communication truly thrives. Where, irrespective of our geographical coordinates, economic status, or cultural backdrop, we can all have an equal piece of the digital pie. So, let's strive to ensure full and effective participation and equal opportunities for all in the digital sphere, ensuring truly holistic intercultural representation.

Ultimately, it comes down to this: there must be no digital 'outsiders'.

The days must end when the digital world is an exclusive club, inaccessible to those on the other side of the digital divide. Equal digital representation isn't just about fairness; it's about creating a truly integrated, global society in an increasingly interconnected world. Achieving this would mean that we've indeed transformed social media platforms into egalitarian spaces, into digital democracies where each netizen, irrespective of their background, can voice their thoughts, share their culture, and participate wholly in the global conversation.

Chapter 11. Looking Ahead: The Future of Social Media and Intercultural Communication

Looking towards the future can evoke an array of emotions, from thrill and anticipation to anxiety and uncertainty. Predicting or gazing into the future becomes even more complex when it revolves around the heady mix of technology, communication, and intercultural dynamics. Nevertheless, our task is to decipher the trends, to predict the possible trajectories, and to elucidate the potentials and challenges that lie ahead in the realm of social media and intercultural communication.

11.1. The Horizon of Technological Developments

At the heart of this discourse is the very platform that enables intercultural communication - technology. Technology will continue to evolve at a swift pace, pushing the bounds of what is currently possible. Artificial Intelligence (AI) is one such frontier technology that will considerably influence the workings of intercultural communication on social media platforms. More specifically, sophisticated language-translation AI systems will remove the literal barriers of communication, implying a future where language will no longer be a hurdle in cross-cultural interactions. This will indeed promote comprehension and thus, more nuanced interaction among cultures.

We should also anticipate enhancements in virtual and augmented reality capabilities, shaping the way we consume and interact with content. A virtual tête-à-tête amidst the setting of an ancient Mayan city, or a tour through the bustling streets of Tokyo, all from the comfort of your home? Owing to these technologies, experiencing various aspects of cultures could become more vivid and immersive, thereby, enriching the process of intercultural learning and exchange.

Another interesting technological development is the rise of blockchain and cryptocurrency. While primarily, these technologies are not directly linked with social media communication, they present considerable potential to impact digital social interactions and thereby, intercultural communications. For instance, NFTs (Non-Fungible Tokens) enabled by blockchain technology could provide an avenue for artists and creators from diverse backgrounds to harness the power of social media and thus, propagate their cultural works globally.

11.2. Social Media Platforms and Their Evolving Role

Not far behind in this race for the future are the social media platforms themselves. Continuous attempts to innovate and adapt to the evolving technology landscape and user preferences are indicative of the directions these platforms might take. We might find ourselves amidst a greater number of context-specific social media platforms, allowing for more targeted intercultural interactions. Imagine a platform dedicated to fostering conversations and interactions around indigenous knowledge systems, or a platform showcasing music and artforms from all around the globe.

The future may also see a shift towards more responsible social media, emphasizing data privacy and user security. This change could foster trust among users, thereby encouraging more honest, open, and meaningful intercultural interactions.

11.3. The Future of Intercultural Communication Dynamics

With the ongoing rapid digital transformation, it's foreseeable that intercultural communication dynamics are bound to evolve. One of the most significant transformations could be an increased democratization of global voices. The egalitarian nature of social media empowers individuals from different parts of the world, breaking down the traditional power hierarchies that have historically shaped media narratives.

As this democratization progresses, it's critical to nurture media literacy further, to ensure the interpretation and creation of cross-cultural content is done with cultural sensitivity and respect. Encouraging individuals to ascend from cultural competence to cultural intelligence - which entails not just knowledge of diverse cultures but the ability to adapt, respect, and appreciate them.

11.4. Challenges and Opportunities

No conversation about the future can be complete without addressing the challenges and opportunities that come with it. As the influence of social media expands, so does its implications for intercultural communication. This increased exposure to diverse cultures can potentially pave the way for a more inclusive, empathetic world. Yet, it can also exacerbate cultural stereotypes and misinformation if not handled responsibly.

Exploring and defining normative behavior and communication in this digital world will pose significant challenges. Crafting an inclusive narrative that respects all cultures while balancing the fine line between freedom of speech and censorship will be crucial in the years to come. Including worldwide perspectives and voices in these conversations will be pivotal to shaping the concept of digital citizenship, ensuring it encompasses a truly global spirit.

Finally, it's vital to remember that access to social media platforms remains unequal across the globe. Bridging this digital divide will require intention, policy support, and technology deployment.

11.5. Conclusion

The future of social media and intercultural communication is indeed a kaleidoscope of emerging technologies, evolving user behaviors, and shifting cultural dynamics. As digital natives of the 21st century, we carry the exciting responsibility and challenge to shape this digital realm into a vibrant platform that empowers cultural exchange and fosters understanding, empathy, and cohesion amongst the global community. The journey may be complex, it may be arduous, but it will undoubtedly add another intriguing chapter to the narrative of human connection and communication.

www.ingramcontent.com/pod-product-compliance
Lightning Source LLC
LaVergne TN
LVHW051626050326
832903LV00033B/4686